cont

G000298744

Art Theory

Art History 17 - 27

Famous Artists 28 - 33

THE COLOUR WHEEL

THE COLOUR WHEEL

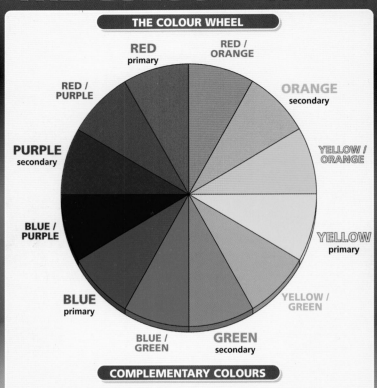

COMPLEMENTARY COLOURS

The colours opposite each other on the wheel are called complementary colours.

RED	is opposite	GREEN
BLUE	is opposite	ORANGE
YELLOW	is opposite	PURPLE

If a colour is surrounded by its complementary colour it will appear stronger and brighter.

TEL 0800 050 5232
www.daydreameducation.co.uk

PRIMARY AND SECONDARY COLOURS

PRIMARY COLOURS

There are **THREE PRIMARY COLOURS.**
These are pure colours which cannot be made by mixing other colours.

RED **YELLOW** **BLUE**

SECONDARY COLOURS

Secondary colours are made by mixing each primary colour with one other primary colour.

PRIMARY **+** **PRIMARY** **=** **SECONDARY**

 + **=**

RED **YELLOW** **ORANGE**

 + **=**

YELLOW **BLUE** **GREEN**

 + **=**

BLUE **RED** **PURPLE**

TERTIARY COLOURS

Tertiary colours contain a mix of all three primary colours.
A primary colour, mixed with its complementary colour equals a tertiary colour.

PRIMARY + COMPLEMENTARY = TERTIARY

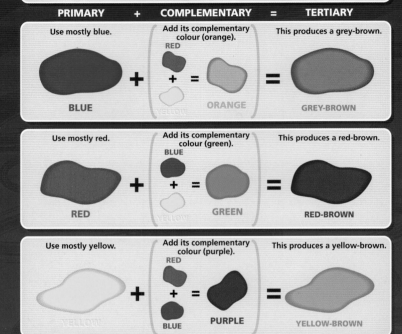

Use mostly blue.

Add its complementary colour (orange).
RED
+
YELLOW

This produces a grey-brown.

BLUE + **ORANGE** = **GREY-BROWN**

Use mostly red.

Add its complementary colour (green).
BLUE
+
YELLOW

This produces a red-brown.

RED + **GREEN** = **RED-BROWN**

Use mostly yellow.

Add its complementary colour (purple).
RED
+
BLUE

This produces a yellow-brown.

YELLOW + **PURPLE** = **YELLOW-BROWN**

By using varying amounts of each colour, an infinite number of shades are possible.
The more colours are mixed on the palette, the
less luminous the result.

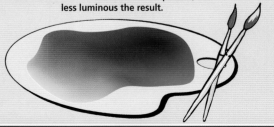

TONE

This tonal scale shows the gradation of dark tones, mid tones and light tones.

It shows the passage from black through grey to white.

DARK ⟶ MID ⟶ LIGHT

TINTING AND SHADING

Tinting and shading refer to making a colour lighter by adding white (tinting) or darker by adding black (shading).

BLUE ⟶ ADDING WHITE

This tonal scale shows the gradation in tone of the colour blue by adding white.

RED ⟶ ADDING BLACK

This tonal scale shows the gradation in tone of the colour red by adding black.

TINTING AND SHADING WITH COLOUR

RED ⟶ ORANGE ⟶ YELLOW

This tonal scale shows the gradation in tone of the orange when mixing different quantities of red and yellow.

CIRCLES AND ELLIPSES

An ellipse is a circle tilted away from you - a circle in perspective.

circle

ellipse

HOW A CIRCLE BECOMES AN ELLIPSE

A circle can be drawn in a square.

By tilting the square, it is now in perspective.

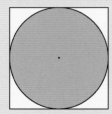

The centre of the square is also the centre of the circle.

The circle has now become an ellipse.

HOW TO DRAW AN ELLIPSE

1. Draw a square in perspective.

2. Find the perspective centre of the square by drawing diagonal lines.

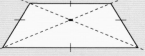

3. Mark the perspective centre of each side of the square.

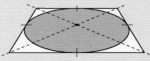

4. Now draw an ellipse so the curve touches each of the four sides.

daydream
education

Tel: 0800 808 8232
www.daydreameducation.co.uk

LIGHT AND SHADE

The above flat (2-dimensional) objects appear solid (3-dimensional)
when drawn in perspective as shown below.

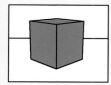  

 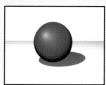 

Light helps show the volume of an object.
When light falls on an object, shadows and highlights occur.

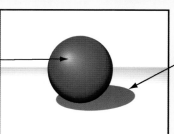

HIGHLIGHTS
occur when light
falls directly on to
an object.

SHADOWS
are caused when
the object blocks
the light.

FORMAL ELEMENTS

The formal elements are the basic components from which two-dimensional designs are composed.

LINE

Connection between two points.

SHAPE

Created by a closed line or by a solid colour.

TEXTURE

Visual and tactile surface.

COLOUR

Primary, secondary, tertiary, complementary colours.

TONE

Shadows, mid-tones, highlights.

PATTERN

Natural, man-made, repeat or mirrored.

daydream

TEL 0800 009 0232
www.daydreameducation.co.uk

LOOKING AT IMAGES

When discussing 2D and 3D work, there are four main elements to consider:

CONTENT

- What is the image about?
- Is it a representational or an abstract piece of work?

Pablo Picasso (1881-1973)
Portrait of Dora Maar (1937)

- Are there any hidden meanings in the picture?

FORM

- What colours have been used?
- Is it realistic, harmonious or contrasting?

Jacoba van Heemskerck (1876-1923)
Landscape (1915)

- Are there any recurrent shapes, lines, forms, patterns or textures?

PROCESS

- How was the piece produced and of what was it made?

Jackson Pollock (1912-1956)
Number 33 (1949)

- What techniques and processes were used?

MOOD

- Does the work capture a mood, feeling or emotion?

Joseph Mallord William Turner (1775-1851)
Pembroke Castle (1801)

- What techniques has the artist used to convey the mood?

PERSPECTIVE

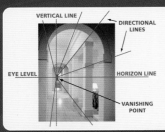

If you stand at one end of a corridor and look down it, you will see the walls and ceiling appear to converge.

If the horizon line, vertical line and directional lines are extended they always meet.

The point at which they converge is known as the **VANISHING POINT**.

This point is at **EYE LEVEL**.

ONE-POINT PERSPECTIVE

One-point perspective is used when standing in front of an object.

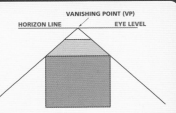

TWO-POINT PERSPECTIVE

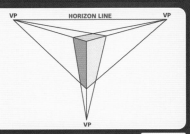

Two-point perspective is used when looking at an object from one corner.

THREE-POINT PERSPECTIVE

Three-point perspective is used when objects are seen from above or below.

PORTRAIT

HOW TO DRAW A PORTRAIT - A STEP BY STEP GUIDE

STEP 1

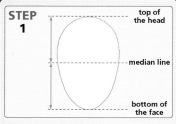

- Draw an egg-shaped oval.
- Split the oval in two halves with a horizontal line (median line).

STEP 2

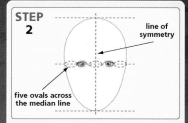

- Draw a vertical line of symmetry.
- Draw 5 ovals across the median line.
- Two of the ovals become the eyes.

STEP 3

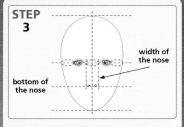

- The nose is the width of the centre oval.
- The base of the nose lies halfway between the median line and the bottom of the face.

STEP 4

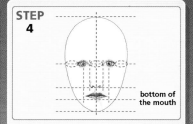

- The mouth lies above a line halfway between the base of the nose and bottom of the face.
- The bottom lip is usually fuller than the top.

STEP 5

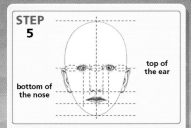

- The ears are bigger than you would imagine.
- They are drawn from the median line to just below the base of the nose line.

STEP 6

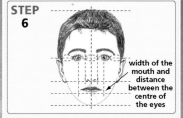

- Add the eyebrows which are thicker in the middle and thinner on the outside of the face.
- Add a hair style of your choice.

PROPORTIONS
OF THE HUMAN FIGURE

Use the height of the head to help you gain the correct proportions for the body.

Most people are around **8 head-lengths** tall.

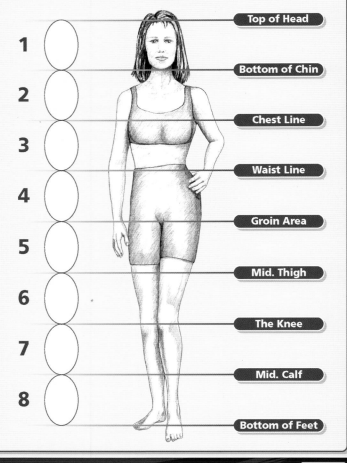

1
2
3
4
5
6
7
8

- Top of Head
- Bottom of Chin
- Chest Line
- Waist Line
- Groin Area
- Mid. Thigh
- The Knee
- Mid. Calf
- Bottom of Feet

SCALING

GRID SYSTEM

To scale a small drawing up to a larger drawing you
use a grid to maintain the correct proportion.

Vincent van Gogh (1853-1890)
Sunflowers (1888)

7cm

5cm

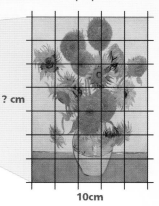

? cm

10cm

The proportions of both
pictures must be the same.

$$\frac{\text{Height (7)}}{\text{Width (5)}} \times \text{New Width (10)}$$

= New Height (14cm)

National Gallery, London, UK / Bridgeman Art Library

DISTORTION

By stretching the same grid system, but dispensing with
the proportion, you can accurately distort an image.

Vincent van Gogh (1853-1890)
Self Portrait (1887)

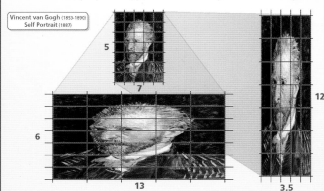

5

7

12

6

13

3.5

Musée d'Orsay, Paris, France / Bridgeman Art Library

STILL LIFE

The term STILL LIFE is used to describe a painting based on a group of inanimate objects.

TRADITIONAL STILL LIFE

Floris van Schooten (fl.1612-1655)
Still Life with Beaker, Cheese, Butter and Biscuits

Traditional Still Life paintings often include an arrangement of objects such as fruit, flowers, bottles and vessels.

ABSTRACT STILL LIFE

Lyubov' Sergeevna Popova (1889-1924)
Italian Still Life (1914)

This is an abstract painting which shows a Still Life where the objects are difficult to recognise.

AUSTRALIAN ABORIGINAL ART

- The Aborigines have occupied Australia for at least 50 thousand years. They have one of the oldest living art traditions in the world.

- The art that the Aborigines show in their paintings often refers to 'The Dreamings': the myths and stories of their ancestors.

Ubiri Rock Art (20th Century)

- The Aborigines used to paint on the walls of rock shelters or on tree bark using natural materials as paint.

Turkey Tolson Tjupurrula (b.c.1938)
Snake Dreaming (1984)

- One characteristic of Aboriginal paintings is simplistic images drawn from above.

Australian School (20th Century)
Kangaroo, Arnhem Land, Northern Territory, Australia (c.1950's)

- Animals are often drawn with their skeleton and inner organs showing. Crosshatching and dotting are added for decoration.

Aboriginal Bark Painting

- Aboriginal paintings depict stories and myths about their ancestors and the creation of their land.

REALISM

- Realism began in the mid-19th century.

- The artists shocked audiences by painting everyday life, rather than the more romantic images that were depicted by earlier painters.

- Realist paintings often depict rural, working-class scenes.

- Jean-François Millet and Gustave Courbet were among the first artists to paint these scenes as they really were.

Jean-François Millet (1814-75)

Jean-François Millet
The Gleaners (1857)

Millet was a French landscape painter. In 1849, he joined the Barbizon school where he produced his most famous paintings of peasants in the fields.

Here Millet has painted a typical rural scene of his time.

Gustave Courbet (1819-77)

Gustave Courbet
The Stone Breakers (1849)

A farmer's son, Courbet learned to paint in the Louvre copying masterpieces. His depiction of manual workers went against the romantic art of the time.

Here Courbet has painted a scene of everyday life showing men repairing a road.

IMPRESSIONISM

The Impressionist movement developed in France around 1869.
The Impressionist painters often painted outside and tried
to depict what they saw at a given moment.

They were especially interested in the effect of changing light, painting
the same subject matter at different times of the day.

Claude Monet (1840-1926)

Claude Monet
The Houses of Parliament, Stormy Sky (1904)

Musee des Beaux-Arts, Lille, France/Bridgeman Giraudon / Lauros

Claude Monet was probably the
most famous of the Impressionist
painters. He painted scenes from
middle-class life and studied how
changing light affected a scene.

Using unmixed colours in short
brush strokes, Monet's technique
epitomised the Impressionist style.

Pierre Auguste Renoir (1841-1919)

Pierre Auguste Renoir
The Luncheon of the Boating Party (1881)

Phillips Collection, Washington DC, USA/Bridgeman Art Library

Recognized as one of the greatest
and most independent painters
of his time, Renoir was more
concerned with the human form,
than with nature or landscapes.

Renoir's style and subject matter
varied throughout his career, his
main subjects being female nudes
and the bustling life of Paris.

POST-IMPRESSIONISM

- Post-Impressionism developed in the late 19th century.

- Post-Impressionists expressed their feelings through bright colours and free brush work.

- They focused on their own personal response to a subject, moving away from the Impressionists' way of painting what they saw.

Vincent van Gogh
Sunflowers (1888)

Vincent van Gogh (1853-90)

Van Gogh had a short, emotionally-troubled career. However, he greatly influenced the Expressionist movement that followed.

Here Van Gogh has used very bright colours and expressive brush strokes.

Neue Pinakothek, Munich, Germany/Bridgeman Art Library

Paul Gauguin
The Yellow Christ (1889)

Paul Gauguin (1848-1903)

Gauguin exhibited with the Impressionists before meeting Van Gogh in 1888. His last days were spent painting in the South Sea Islands.

In this painting, Gauguin used large, flat areas of unrealistic colour, a feature that influenced modern art.

Albright Knox Art Gallery, Buffalo New York, USA/Bridgeman Art Library

POINTILLISM

- Pointillism is a technique of painting associated above all with the artist Georges Seurat.

- Pointillism is named after the French word for painting in dots.

- Instead of mixing colours on the palette, the artist applies pure, unmixed colours in small dots or dashes.

Georges Seurat (1859-91)

Georges Seurat
Sunday Afternoon on the Island of
La Grande Jatte (1884-86)

Seurat was the leader of the Pointillist movement. During his short life, he studied the effects of tone in his many drawings, then concentrated on colour theory in his Pointillist works.

This is Seurat's most famous painting. He spent two years filling the large canvas with small dots.

Art Institute of Chicago, IL, USA / Bridgeman Art Library

Paul Signac (1863-1935)

Paul Signac
Entrance to the Port of Marseille

Signac was hugely influenced by Seurat. He was the main theorist of Pointillism. Later, he moved on to painting in small squares of colour and a more spontaneous style in watercolour.

This painting shows a typical Signac scene of boats in a harbour.

Musee Cantini, Marseille, France / Bridgeman Art Library
©ADAGP, Paris and DACS, London 2002

EXPRESSIONISM

- The Expressionist movement developed during the late 19th and early 20th centuries.

- Expressionists strove to express feelings and emotions rather than to depict reality or nature.

- The painters often captured deep emotions which evoke feelings of death and suffering.

- In the paintings, the subject is often exaggerated and distorted using harsh, bold colours and thick paint to convey emotions.

Edvard Munch
Anxiety (1894)

Edvard Munch (1863-1944)

Edvard Munch's paintings often include such themes as misery, sickness and death.

'Anxiety' was one of a series of paintings related to 'The Scream' which was influenced by a frightening experience Munch had whilst out walking.

Ernst Ludwig Kirchner
Street Scene

Ernst Ludwig Kirchner (1880-1938)

Ernst Kirchner was one of several Expressionist painters who were influenced by Berlin's underworld.

This painting shows a typical Kirchner scene of Berlin's underworld.

FAUVISM

- Fauvism developed in the early 20th century with Henri Matisse being the leader of the group.

- The Fauvists used bright, strong colours, simplified with bold surface patterns. They did not obey the rules of perspective.

- The pure colours the Fauvists typically used were often squeezed on to the canvas straight from the tube.

Henri Matisse (1869-1954)

The Roofs of Collioure (1905)

Matisse conveyed emotional expression through the use of colour and form. He found international acclaim during his lifetime, unlike most artists.

This painting shows Matisse's use of vivid colour, simplified shape and surface pattern.

Hermitage, St. Petersburg, Russia / Bridgeman Art Library
© Succession H. Matisse / DACS 2003

André Derain (1880-1954)

The Turning Road, L'Estaque (1906)

Derain's early work followed the Fauvist style. From 1908, his work had many other influences, including Cézanne, Cubism and Classical French Art.

Derain's painting shows distorted perspectives and unrestrained brushwork.

Museum of Fine Arts, Houston, Texas, USA/Bridgeman Art Library Gift of Audrey Jones Beck

© ADAGP, Paris and DACS, London 2002

CUBISM

- Cubism developed between 1907 and 1914 and was greatly influenced by Cézanne and Primitive Art.
- The two artists chiefly associated with Cubism were Pablo Picasso and Georges Braque.
- The Cubist shows his subject from many different perspectives, angles and viewpoints.
- Collage and limited colours, especially browns and greys, were often used.

Pablo Picasso
Portrait of Ambroise Vollard (1909)

Pablo Picasso (1881-1973)

Picasso experimented with many styles. He is the most famous and influential artist of the 20th century. Along with Braque he developed Cubism.

A typical Cubist portrait in greys and browns.

Pushkin Museum, Moscow, Russia / Bridgeman Art Library
©Succession Picasso / DACS 2002

Georges Braque
Still Life with a Harp and Violin (1912)

Georges Braque (1882-1963)

Braque started painting in the Fauvist style, then in 1909 he met Picasso. They worked closely together developing Cubism until the beginning of the First World War.

After 1918, he worked in various styles until his death in 1963.

A Still Life showing typical cubist shapes.

Kustsammlung Nordrhein-Westfalen, Dusseldorf, Germany / Bridgeman Art Library ©ADAGP, Paris and DACS, London 2002

FUTURISM

- Futurism developed at the beginning of the 20th century.
- Futurist artists attempted to show continuous movement in one picture.
- The artists focused upon representing the machine and motion.
- The result sometimes looks like a series of photographs taken in quick succession.

Umberto Boccioni (1882-1916)

Umberto Boccioni
The City Rises (1911)

Boccioni was the leader of the Futurist movement in Italy. He felt artists should move away from the past and represent the movement and speed of modern civilisation.

This painting shows a city with new industrial construction in progress.

The brushstrokes give the painting energy, for example, showing the twisting figures of the workmen.

Giacomo Balla (1871-1958)

Giacomo Balla
Dynamism of a Dog on a Lead (1912)

Balla started and finished his career with representational painting. However, from 1910 - 1930, he followed the Futurist movement.

This painting was inspired by a photograph showing the movement of a wealthy lady taking her dog for a walk.

SURREALISM

- Surrealism was an artistic movement that developed in the early 1920s.

- Surrealist painters were influenced by the unconscious mind. They explored dreams and dream imagery.

- This resulted in many Surrealist painters using realistic images and objects but in strange and irrational ways.

Giorgio de Chirico (1888-1978)

Giorgio de Chirico
Disquieting Muses (1925)

De Chirico gave great impetus to the surrealist movement, and was an influence on other surrealists such as Salvador Dali and Yves Tanguy.

Here is a typical De Chirico painting showing strange faceless mannequins, a technique he used from 1915 - 1925.

Private Collection / Bridgeman Art Library / Credit: Peter Willi
© DACS 2002

Salvador Dali (1904-89)

Salvador Dali
The Persistence of Memory (1931)

Dali's paintings depict dream imagery and everyday objects in unexpected forms.

In this painting Dali presents a fantasy in a realistic, academic style.

© Salvador Dali / Gala-Salvador Dali Foundation / DACS, London 2002
Museum of Modern Art, New York, USA / Bridgeman Art Library

POP ART

- The 'Pop Art' movement occurred in the 1950s and 1960s and demonstrated bold imagery with brash, heightened colour.

- The Pop Art style derived from everyday objects, items of mass culture, such as comic strip panels, soup cans, beer bottles and road signs.

Campbell's Soup Can (1962)

ANDY WARHOL (1928-1987)

Warhol was the most influential Pop Artist. He used the silkscreen process to transfer photographic images onto canvas.

He used images of celebrities and mass-produced, commercial products.

In The Car (1963)

ROY LICHTENSTEIN (1923-1997)

Lichtenstein is famed for his paintings based on comic strips, often depicting tense, dramatic situations.

He restricted himself to using primary colours, black and white.

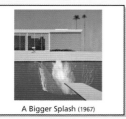

A Bigger Splash (1967)

DAVID HOCKNEY (b. 1937)

David Hockney is the most highly-publicised, British, post-war artist.

Hockney's popularity stems from his flair, wit and versatility in experimenting with painting, photography and film.

CÉZANNE

PAUL CÉZANNE (1839-1906)

- Cézanne was a French, Post-Impressionist painter often referred to as 'the father of modern art'.

- His works and ideas influenced the development of many artists including Pablo Picasso and Henri Matisse and art movements such as Cubism and Fauvism.

Boy with Skull (1896-98)

- Cézanne moved to Paris from Aix-en-Provence in 1861. Here he met Pissarro and other Impressionists.

Bibemus Quarry (1898)

- This painting demonstrates how he took the influence of painting outside, of colour and lighting, from Impressionism.

The Gulf of Marseilles seen from L'Estaque (c.1883)

- Cézanne produced many landscapes and still-life paintings in his lifetime.

Apples and Oranges (1895-1900)

- It was only around 1895 that his work gained the recognition it deserved.

MONET

CLAUDE MONET (1840-1926)

- Monet was a French painter regarded as the leader of the Impressionist movement.
- Monet perfected a technique of working in the open air, capturing the changing effects of natural light.

- Monet worked quickly creating a spontaneous effect without reworking the paint.

Bathers at La Grenouillere (1869)

- He often applied unmixed paint with small strokes.

- He often layered wet paint upon wet paint to create a blurred effect.

Impression: Sunrise, Le Havre (1872)

- Monet avoided the use of black and earthy colours, using complementary colours in their place.

Waterlilies (1903)

- In his later style, he began to concentrate on painting a single subject at different times of the day or seasons of the year.

Waterlilies (1903)

- Monet constructed a water garden; painting the lily pond occupied him until his death.

VAN GOGH

VINCENT VAN GOGH (1853-1890)

- Van Gogh was a Dutch painter, now one of the most popular of the Post-Impressionist painters. He had a short and emotionally troubled career.

- Only when Van Gogh was 27 did he become a full-time artist, leaving behind his career in the church.

- Van Gogh worked with the painter Paul Gauguin, but a conflict of personalities led to an argument after which Van Gogh cut off part of his ear.

- Shortly afterwards, he committed himself to the mental asylum in which he died.

Two Peasants Planting Potatoes (1885)

- 'Two Peasants Planting Potatoes' was typical of his early paintings, where he used dark colours in a Realist style.

Van Gogh's Bedroom at Arles (1889)

- In 1888, Van Gogh moved to Arles in the South of France where some of his most famous works were painted.

Sunflowers (1888)

- Van Gogh's works show his expressive and emotive use of brilliant colour and energetic application of paint.

Vincent's Chair (1888)

- His paintings were highly textured and heavily built-up with paint layers.

PICASSO

PABLO PICASSO (1881-1973)

- Pablo Picasso was a Spanish painter and sculptor, now considered the greatest artist of the 20th century.

- Picasso experimented with many styles creating more than 20,000 works of art.

THE BLUE PERIOD (1901-1904)

- Various shades of blue dominated Picasso's work during this period.

Old Jew with a Boy (1903)

- His paintings expressed human misery, depicting beggars, alcoholics and prostitutes.

THE ROSE PERIOD (1904-1905)

- Many of his subjects were drawn from the circus.

Acrobat and Young Harlequin (1905)

- Influenced by a happy relationship, Picasso changed his palette to pinks and reds.

CUBISM

- Influenced by Paul Cézanne and primitive art, Picasso helped develop Cubism.

Seated Woman Playing the Mandolin (1911)

- Cubism involved the breaking down and analysing of form, showing the subject matter from many different perspectives.

SCULPTURE

- Picasso created sculptures as well as paintings.

Head of a Woman (1909)

- The bronze bust of Fernande Olivier, above, demonstrates his skill in handling three-dimensional form.

MATISSE

HENRI MATISSE (1869-1954)

- Matisse is often regarded as the most important French painter of the 20th century.

- As leader of the Fauvist movement, he conveyed emotional expression through the use of colour and form.

Parrot Tulips II (1905)

The Roofs of Collioure (1905)

- He was greatly influenced by the Pointillist painters who applied pure, unmixed colours in small dots or dashes.

- He added to this technique by changing the small dots or dashes into broader strokes.

La Musique (1939)

Blue Nude III (1952)

- His style changed to a preference for simplified areas of pure colours, strong pattern and flat shapes, as well as abandoning three-dimensional effects.

- In his later years, as he became much weaker, he cut out shapes of brightly-coloured paper, collaging them into fantastic abstract designs.

DALI

SALVADOR DALI (1904-1989)

- Dali was an an eccentric Spanish painter. In 1929, he joined the French Surrealist group.

- As well as painting, Dali worked in many mediums: he designed stage sets, clothing, jewellery and even surrealist films.

Persistence of Memory (1931)

Swans Reflecting Elephants (1937)

- The painting 'Persistence of Memory', showing limp watches, is one of the most well-known surrealist works.

- Dali often depicted dream imagery and everyday objects in unexpected forms, tapping into his unconscious mind.

The Hallucinogenic Toreador (1968-1970)

Sacrament of the Last Supper (1955)

- Rich colour, detail and the use of repeated images in this painting show the development of Dali's surrealist style.

- Dali returned to the Catholic faith of his childhood and his later paintings were often based on religious themes.

subjects include:

Art & Design
Pocket Posters
G.C.S.E.

Business Studies
Pocket Posters
G.C.S.E.

English Pocket Posters
Key Stage 2
Key Stage 3

Geography
Pocket Posters
Key Stage 3

I.C.T. Pocket Posters
Key Stage 2
G.C.S.E.

Maths Pocket Posters
Key Stage 2
Key Stage 3

Music Pocket Posters
Key Stage 2
Key Stage 3

Physical Education
Pocket Posters
G.C.S.E.

R.E. Pocket Posters
Key Stage 2
Key Stage 3

Science Pocket Posters
Key Stage 2
Key Stage 3

**Please see website
for details of our
Pocket Poster
Packs.**